i

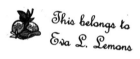

This belongs to
Eva L. Lemons

This belongs to
Eva L. Lemons

A

Woman's

Place

Leading Ladies Speak

Anthology Compiled by

Crystal Jones & Joceline Bronson

Destiny House Publishing, LLC

Detroit, MI

A Woman's Place

Leading Ladies Speak

ISBN: 1936867060 and the ISBN 13 is 9781936867066

Published by Destiny House Publishing, LLC

Edited by Destiny House Publishing, LLC

Unless otherwise stated, all scripture quotations are from the Holy Bible, King James Version

Scripture references that do not have the Bible version noted are the author's paraphrase.

Cover design. Editing and Publication Layout:

Destiny House Publishing, LLC

Printed in the United States of America

For information:

Destiny House Publishing, LLC

www.destinyhousepublishing.com

email: inquiry@destinyhousepublishing.com

P.O. Box 19774 - Detroit, MI 48219 888.890.5444

- Contents -

- Contents -

Dedications

A Woman's Place is dedicated to the amazing women of God all around the world who yearn to offer the Lord their gifts and talents.

Acknowledgments

First and foremost we acknowledge our faithful Lord and Savior, Jesus Christ. Without Him none of this would even be possible. Everything we do is because of you. Thank you for extending your gift of salvation to us. It is a privilege and an honor to serve you and to live for you.

Apostle Oscar Jones, you have been my (Crystal Jones) anchor. I love you so much. Thank you for your unceasing support. You are the beat of my heart.

Charity Dean for her diligent labor in leading the editing for this project. Thank you for your tedious work. You are a gem.

Kyria Jones who helped out wherever needed including producing spreadsheets to make the process smoother.

And of course, acknowledgment goes to all of the leading ladies who contributed to this work:

Julia Bibbs

Angela Bradley

Joceline Bronson

Tonya Dillard

Sharee Hall

Crystal Jones

Cynthia McKinney

Nina Pringle

Michelle Stapleton-Morris

Angela Thibeaux

Claudia Thomas

Doreen Thornton

Torrona Tillman

Chapter 1: A Love Letter to God's Daughters

My Dearest Daughters,

Before you knew me, I loved you. And I chose you to be mine. There is no one else on this earth exactly like you. I created you to be one of a kind. No one else can be you. So be you. Don't seek after the gifts, talents, or positions of others.

I make all things beautiful in my time. You are meticulously and intricately designed by me. So when seeking your purpose and destiny you need to come to me. Others will underestimate who I have chosen you to be. So don't seek affirmation from them. Trust me to reveal it to you.

You are 100% accepted by me. You don't have to fit the mold of others expectations. Let no one else define you. I Love you with all my heart. In fact, I think about you all the time. My thoughts of you are numbered as the sand. I never misunderstand your thoughts, your motives, and the things you say.

Forgive those who have interfered with your purpose. You will have to continue to forgive throughout your entire journey on the earth. And you can, because I offer this abundance of mercy to you, everyday.

Walk closely with me. Hold my hand and follow my instructions. May you never feel out of place. Because I have reserved a special place for you. Your place as a woman of God is in my kingdom, in my presence, in my will, and in my heart. Take your place.

Always,

The Lover of Your Soul

Reflections:

Can you believe that God loves and favors you? What if the image that God has of you matched who you really are? What would that look like?

_____

_____

_____

_____

_____

_____

Scriptures to Ponder:

Everyone who is called by my name, who I created for my glory, whom I formed and made. Isaiah 43:7 NIV

How precious to me are your thoughts, O God! How vast is the sum of them! Were I to count them, they would outnumber the grains of sand. When I awake, I am still with you. Psalm 139:17-18 NIV

What is your response to this letter? Write back to the Lord.

_____

_____

_____

_____

_____

_____

_____

_____

_____

_____

_____

_____

_____

_____

Chapter 2-

You Can Have New Beginnings; God Did!

By Prophetess Doreen Thornton

Prophetess Doreen Thornton

Prophetess Doreen Thornton, Pastor is the mother of four daughter's and six grandchildren. Prophetess Doreen serves as Senior Pastor of A Place To Pray International Deliverance Ministries, and Pastor/Board Member of Wign-TV the Women's Internet Gospel Network. She has a passion and love for soul winning and ministering to the whole man.

Wign-TV the Women's Internet
Gospel Network
2000 Town Center, Suite 1900
Southfield, Michigan. 48075
248-979-0975

You Can Have New Beginnings; God did!

My beautiful sisters, according to John 3:16, God's desire is that you believe he loves you and sent his Son Jesus Christ to give his life for yours to save you. The plan of God for our lives is not designed to destroy us. Jeremiah 29:11,"For I know the thoughts that I think toward you", saith the LORD, "thoughts of peace, and not of evil, to give you an expected end."

In the United States, women are blessed beyond measure with the opportunity to educate ourselves and have extraordinary families and careers. We live in a land flowing with milk and honey. Thank you, Jesus for God's abundance and liberation to pursue the visions and dreams that God has given to us, without a lot of social or religious hindrances. However, some Christian women experience frustration in their walk with God due to a "lack of knowledge."

Not knowing, understanding or acknowledging God's perfect will or plan for your life will cause an imbalance in your personal growth and will affect everyone around you. A woman can have greatness that may include higher education and a successful corporate career or business and live empty, unfulfilled, and spiritually impoverished. According to Proverbs 11:1, "A false balance is abomination to the LORD: but a just weight is his delight." As wise women, we should seek God for the blueprints for our lives and the life of our families. "Wisdom is the principal thing; therefore

9

get wisdom: and with all thy getting get understanding." Proverbs 4:7

How can you obtain a spiritual understanding of God's will for your life? Seven times in the Book of Revelations 2:7-3:33, Jesus said, "Let him hear what the Spirit saith unto the churches." God is speaking to his daughter twenty-four hours a day, seven days a week; in His written word, the Holy Bible. According to the book of Hebrews, it is Jesus that we must seek out to speak to us, Hebrew 1:1-2, "God, who at sundry times and in divers manners spake in time past unto the fathers by the prophets. Hath in these last days spoken unto us by his Son, whom he hath appointed heir of all things, by whom also he made the worlds."

We are living in the age of the resurrection of the Prophetic Anointing. However some of us have acquired a dependency on the gift of the prophet in a man or woman and not the gift giver, Jesus Christ. According to the book of Ephesians 4:8-12, Jesus gave gifts unto men, apostles, prophets, evangelist, pastor and teacher, to perfect the saints, to work ministry and edify the body of Christ. The gifts in man were never intended by God to replace Jesus Christ or our need to abide in Jesus alone.

Apostle John gets an understanding of who to worship and why: Revelation 19:10, "And I fell at his feet to worship him. And he said unto me, See thou do it not: I am thy fellow servant, and of thy brethren that have the testimony of Jesus: worship God: for the testimony of Jesus is the spirit of prophecy."

We honor the men and women that serve God with "double honor." However we do not worship them, or put our total dependency and trust in them, we follow them as they "follow Christ." And rely 100% on the Word of God that comes out of their mouth, with an understanding that Jesus Christ is the "Word of God." John 1:1 "And Jesus is "Spirit of Prophecy."" Revelations 19:10,"And all spiritual gifts come from Jesus." No man or women can or should take the credit for what cost God his only Son, and cost his Son Jesus his life and blood; that he gave for his love for man and to heal the sins of the world.

Nicodemus, a ruler of the Jews, honored Jesus by calling him, Rabbi, which means lord or teacher, and he also acknowledged the miracles Jesus performed. However Jesus did not respond to the words that could have flattered him. Jesus gave Nicodemus knowledge of a new eternal beginning he could have with him. John 3:3, "Jesus answered and said unto him, Verily, verily, I say unto thee, Except a man be born again, he cannot see the kingdom of God."

In order to see or enter into the Kingdom of God, one must first be born again. You cannot comprehend what Jesus Christ is saying to you if you are not born again. The carnal mind is not subject to God and is the enemy of our new beginning. If we want to receive the benefits of God's thoughts and plans for our life we must first become his daughter. John 1:12, "But as many as received him, to them gave he power to become the sons of God, even to them that believe on his name."

Apostle Paul said "let this mind be in you, which was also in Christ Jesus." Philippians 2:5,"With the mind of Christ activated in us, we are stimulated with, creation, new birth, manifestation, and have a right to subdue and have dominion over the earth."

Instructions were given to Joshua for the new beginning of the children of Israel. Joshua 1:8, "This book of the law shall not depart out of thy mouth; but thou shalt meditate therein day and night, that thou mayest observe to do according to all that is written therein: for then thou shalt make thy way prosperous, and then thou shalt have good success."

Prosperity and good success only comes from meditating and obeying the word of God. Press into prayer and fasting. It is the will of Christ that we accomplish Greater Works than himself, to the glory of God.

God wants you to start over, freshly forgiven. You are the glory of God and he wants to show you off and give you double for your trouble, stay encouraged.

Reflections:

Is your prayer life what it should be? Do you consistently study the word of God? Do you receive God's love and mercy?

_____

_____

_____

_____

_____

_____

Scripture to Ponder:

It is of the LORD's mercies that we are not consumed, because his compassions fail not. They are new every morning: great is thy faithfulness. Lamentations 3:22

What do you need for a new beginning?

_____

_____

_____

_____

_____

_____

_____

_____

_____

_____

_____

_____

A Fresh Start:

If you desire a personal relationship with him, a simple prayer is all that is required.   It is as simple as **ABC**:

Acknowledge that you are a sinner:

"Lord, I recognize that I have broken your laws. My sins have separated me from you.

Believe that He is the only begotten son of the Father

"I believe that your Son, Jesus Christ, was sent to die for my sins. He was resurrected from the dead and now extends to me new life. He reigns as Lord of my life.

Commit to Change:

"I invite your son to rule in my heart. Please send your Holy Spirit to help me obey you . I choose to live for you for the rest of my life.

In Jesus' precious name I pray, Amen.

If you chose to make a commitment or recommitment to Christ, welcome to God's Family. You are now positioned to receive all rights, benefits and privileges that belong to the children of the King. Find a Christian Bible-believing church to help you grow in your relationship with the Lord.

There are several churches represented in this book from various parts of the United States. Feel free to contact any of them to help you get the fresh start that you need.

- Chapter 3 -

Sleeping Beauty
By Crystal Jones

Prophetess Crystal Jones

Prophetess Crystal is the true love of Apostle Oscar Jones, they celebrate more than 30 years of marriage. Crystal is the loving mother of 5 adult children and 2 bonus children (in-laws) and the beaming grandmother of 6.

Along with her husband, Prophetess Crystal oversees **Greater Works Family Ministries**, is co-founder of **Marriage For A Lifetime Ministries** and the two are apostolic overseers to **Agape International Association of Churches and Para-churches**. They have a unique Aquila & Priscilla anointing where they minister together as one voice.

Crystal is wildly in love with her Lord and Savior, Jesus Christ and is fully committed to her relationship with Him.

Marriage For A Lifetime Ministries

P.O. Box 24906 Oakland, CA 94623
888.884.3556 www.marriage4alifetime.org
jones@marriage4alifetime.org

Sleeping Beauty

I want to tell you a story. It's a true story about you. You are Beauty, in search of significance. But before I can get to the story, I must prepare you. You die in this story. There is devastation, heartache and pain that will hit your life. But don't lose heart; it doesn't end there.

Follow me, as I introduce you to Beauty.

Once upon a time, God created man. And man was complete in himself. He was created in God's holy image. The Lord saw that it was not good for the man to be alone. So he pulled Beauty out of him. She is the softer side of God. She is the grace and compassion of God. She is woman. Beauty was created on and in purpose. When God made male and female, he spoke purpose and destiny to **them** both. (Genesis 2:27-28)

But, somehow, as with most stories, something went wrong. God gave man and woman gifts. Unfortunately, man thought it was wrong for the woman to unwrap her gifts. He could use his. But she dare not use hers. His thoughts were that she was to sit still and quiet. God would not receive from her because she was born lesser than him. (As if her gender were a curse)

Satan hates all of mankind. And he especially detests the feminine man. She was created with a capacity to give birth, not only in the physical but she is able to give birth to dreams, vision, and destiny. She is his antithesis. Feminine man represents life. Satan represents death. She multiplies, He divides. She is a builder. He is a destroyer. She is his enemy and he is hers. And the two have been at odds since the beginning of time.

Satan's primary purpose throughout cultures, religions and generations has been to shut down the woman. He has something against Beauty. So he whispers to man, "Do not allow her to give birth. Do not allow her to reproduce. Do not allow her to speak. Keep her tied up. Keep her out of purpose".

Purpose Aborted

Whenever we operate outside of purpose, something in us dies. We lose desire and passion and our ability to dream. The Bible says that without a vision, the people perish. A woman must have a vision of her future. That vision speaks to her purpose. If she is not allowed to do what God calls her to do, she ventures off into something else. Something other than what God intended. And that something else becomes lethal.

Beauty hurts. She is wounded. She gets entangled in self-pity, fear, anger or revenge. Beauty gets lost in her sin sickness. She tries to find fulfillment in relationships. She wanders aimlessly from one relationship to another looking for love, acceptance and approval. She is physically abused and she takes it. She is verbally abused and she receives it. She is emotionally abused and she seems to need it. Rejected, offended and broken, she sees nothing valuable in herself. She is living in a house of mirrors with distorted reflections. *And she bleeds from the inside out.*

But wait... you are Beauty.

Fear and intimidation are the weapons that the enemy uses against you. Fear won't allow you to trust. Intimidation immobilizes you. You are unsure of who you really are.   You become a mere fragment of your true self; never able to see into your future. Your view is skewed. You can't imagine that God could somehow use you. So you accept this broken picture of yourself. And you tell yourself that these bruises, these wounds and the scars they left, is who you really are: bitter, self-conscious, controlling, angry, prideful and vengeful.   A bundle of mess; all because Beauty took a detour from her God-ordained purpose.

The death of Beauty

And without warning, Beauty dies. When did she first die? Beauty died in the garden, when she believed Satan's first lie. Many more lies have been told since then. He hasn't stop lying. He keeps whispering in your ear. "Hath God not said...?" And he fills in the rest. Because you believe his lies, you sit on the sidelines never

21

hearkening to what God has spoken. You give ear to the wrong voice. And you never take dominion. You are no longer fruitful. You aren't doing what you were born to do.

And so your heart stops beating.

Let's take a look at scripture at another daughter who was near death. St Mark 5:21-22 A certain church leader was desperate. He came and fell at the feet of Jesus because his baby was dying. His daughter, the one that carried his heart. He knew her only hope was if Jesus would come and lay his hands on her. So he made the trek to find him. And he did.

There is a difference in your story. Your Dad is seeking you. He, who is, the Chief Physician only needs an encounter with Beauty. Sadly, Most times, Beauty flees.

The funeral

St. Mark 5:35 While Jesus was still speaking, some people came from the house of Jairus, the synagogue leader. "Your daughter is dead," they said. "Why bother the teacher anymore?"

Death tipped in when it seemed as if God wasn't watching. Even in some of your lives, some of you have died. You've lost meaning. Death slithered in. You've felt like you've wasted most of your life and now you are just too old to do anything worthwhile for God? Or you've been somewhere waiting to exhale; hoping a husband would give meaning to your life. Some of you have expended your energy on bad relationships and you feel like you have nothing left to give. Others have given up a long time ago because you feel you've just done too much wrong. "If God ever forgives me, how will I ever forgive myself?" And so Beauty proceeds through life like a zombie. Just going through the motions. Just making it. Just getting by. Never aspiring to do anything big. Just wanting to get through another day. Often Beauty feels lonely, forgotten and forsaken; like she doesn't even matter. She needs to breathe. She is dead to life. And so they prepare her funeral.

St. Mark 5:38 When they came to the home of the synagogue leader, Jesus saw a commotion, with people crying and wailing loudly.

It's odd, how people seem to rally around during a funeral. Some of which you haven't seen in years. They come out of the woodworks. Death seems to invite them. People who didn't even like you will come to your funeral. All your haters, forsakers, and naysayers show up. That's just how it is. They come to make sure that you are dead. Some come to see who else will be there, as if it's some kind of party. They celebrate your tragedy.

Some applaud your woundedness. The "I told you so's" hover over your head. They wag their heads and point their fingers.

They don't understand that it's not the end of your story.

The interruption

When Jesus reaches the girl, funeral preparations
are already made. The people have already
gathered.

A funeral is the closing chapter over a person's
life. All has been said and done; it is the last
rites. You may have had situations where people
have had *their* last words over you. They have
already counted you out. They step over you and
leave you for dead; the haters laugh. Your
enemies nod.

But God has a pesky habit of stepping in and
interrupting funerals (remember Lazarus John
11:43). Stop your singing. Stop the procession.

St. Mark 5:37 *He did not let anyone follow him
except Peter, James and John the brother of
James.* ** *³⁹ He went in and said to them, "Why all
this commotion and wailing? The child is not
dead, but asleep."*

When others have counted you out, God said
Beauty is only sleeping. She's not dead. Even
when they laugh at the word that God speaks
over you. He continues towards you.

St. Mark 5:41 *He took her by the hand and said
to her, "Talitha koum!" (which means, "Little girl,
I say to you, get up!").*

Arise my daughter. Get up. Life defies death.
Jesus said I am the way the truth and the Life.

His Life saves your life. He extends to you beauty for your awful ashes. And while others may count you out, It's not over 'til God says it's over. They may have given up on you. You may have even given up on yourself. But God says, "**Get up my sleeping beauty. Your Prince has come."**

The victory

Immediately the girl stood up and walked around (she was twelve years old). At this they were completely astonished. St. Mark 5:42

God is going to astonish those around you. You are not defined by the pain and trials you have endured. This is not your authentic self. You haven't quite met her yet. Real Beauty is free, adventurous, joyful, bold, and passionate. You are just like your Daddy.

There have been others who were found dead and the Prince presented them alive. And look what happened.

He presented her alive (Acts 9:41) And it was known throughout all Joppa: and many believed in the Lord Acts 9:42,

Because you are being raised from your dead state, many will believe in God. Your testimony will cause many to come into the kingdom. Men and women will be rallied to God. Unwrap your gifts. Celebrate who God has called you to be.

You are chosen by God to be His darling daughter. You are a peculiar or rare treasure. He has caused you to triumph in Christ Jesus. You will win over your enemies. You overcome by the blood of the Lamb and the words of your testimony. Because the Greater lies within you, you must open your mouth. You must walk out His plan for your life. You are not just a survivor, but more than a conqueror. Somebody needs to hear your story. Just like the woman who encountered Jesus at the well (St. John 4). He didn't disqualify her because of her past. He freed her and let her do what she was born to do. And her testimony converted an entire city. In the same way, God frees you to do what you were born to do. Beauty, you do have a place in the Kingdom of God. Your place is in His will, in his purpose, and in his plan. Use whatever gifting God has given you, Daughter. Don't get sidetracked or distracted by the cares and sins of the world. Get in position.

Awaken daughters. You've been kissed by your prince. It's your time.

~~~~

Reflections:

What has happened in your life that has caused a spiritual death in purpose? What relationships hinder your relationship with the Lord?

_____

_____

_____

_____

_____

Do you see yourself as beautiful? Do you see yourself as God's daughter or his servant?

_____

_____

_____

_____

_____

_____

_____

Scriptures to Ponder:

He has made everything beautiful in his time.
Ecclesiastes 3:11

I am fearfully and wonderfully made.
Psalm 139:NIV

What are your gifts, talents, and abilities?

_____

_____

_____

_____

_____

Write the vision of your future.

_____

_____

_____

_____

_____

_____

_____

Chapter 4
Holding On While Growing In the Kingdom
By Prophetess Julia Bibbs

Prophetess Julia Bibbs

Prophetess Julia Hall Bibbs is the loving wife of Minister Carlos V. Bibbs for 10 years. God has given and entrusted them with a precious son, Joshua Jordan Bibbs. They reside in Olive Branch, MS. Desiring to usher people into their God given destinies and ordained purposes, the Bibbs serve in ministry at Manifold Wisdom COGIC in Hernando, MS. They faithfully embrace their call to love, help and direct God's people to their destiny.

A Woman With A Destiny Ministries
7964 Camptown Lane
Olive Branch, MS 38654
www.julia.bibbs@yahoo.com

Holding On While Growing In the Kingdom

Often times in our walk with the Lord, as we grow in our spiritual purpose and our divine destiny, we come up against trials such as: sickness, lack in finances, depression, insecurity and low self esteem. It seems hard to hold on to what God has promised to us that has not yet come to pass. We know we have an anointing, a spiritual purpose, and a divine destiny to grow in the kingdom of God, to do the kingdom work of the Lord. I am reminded of Philippians 3:13-14, "Brethren, I do not count myself to have apprehended; but one thing I do, forgetting those things which are behind and reaching forward to those things which are ahead, I press toward the goal for the prize of the upward call of God in Christ Jesus." NKJV

This verse gave me the strength to hold on many days, forgetting yesterday's pains, putting them behind me and pressing to grow in my healing through the word of God. It gave me strength when I couldn't see my way through sickness. I was diagnosed with Lupus and Rheumatoid Arthritis 12 years ago. I have been holding on to God with this sickness and yet preaching for the Lord's kingdom in the earth. Many times I thought to give up, but I knew I was chosen for a purpose to do the will of God in the earth. I had to get a renewed mindset in order to hold on, while I was growing in kingdom of the Lord. I had to learn how to be content in whatever state I was in. In order for me to conquer this thought pattern, I had to put off the old mindset and connect with the new mindset as a woman, renewed in knowledge according to the image of Him who created her. I had to grasp this mindset in order to move forward in the kingdom while in the process of growing, even though my body was weak and pain was all over it.

By allowing the Lord to change my mentality, now I could realize that God had given me a place in the kingdom to do His divine will. Having confidence in knowing God, has positioned me in a place of growing and holding on. And with this new mindset, I was able to know that no power from the enemy or any person could move me from the place God has chosen for me. *Now we as people can give up our place by not obeying the will of God for our life.* However no one can take it from us.

 The Lord has given me strength to endure this process of holding on to grow in maturity in the spirit. I often think about the scripture; "The joy of the Lord is my strength". If I had not held on with my faith and believing the words of God, where would I have been in my health and in my spiritual walk with God?

Yet growing in the word of God to a mature state to handle this new chapter of my life, motherhood, was another challenge for me, as I was still holding on. I had to grow even more, because now it was more than just my husband

and I. We were about to face a miracle gift that God had bestowed upon us, where man had said it wasn't possible. I remember it like it was just a few minutes ago. After we had gotten the report from the doctor that it wasn't possible for us to have a child, my husband spoke these words to me, "Whose report will you believe?" It was like God Himself spoke directly to me and all I could do was cry. Through my husband, God was letting me know, that with the carnal eyes it doesn't look possible, but He was going to grant me a child. I had to hold on to the promise while doing His will for the kingdom. God said that He would grant me all the desires of my heart. I had to hold on to the word that said, "Where it is impossible with man, all things are possible with God". I had to put my faith in action with the Word of God. I had to believe that it wouldn't return to me void but that it would prosper what it had been sent to do.

Then our precious son arrived. I am a wife, a mother and a prophetess chosen by God but still wondering how I am I going to continue to grow in the kingdom without letting go.

I was called by the Lord to consecrate and fast to loose strongholds of doubt and unbelief that were trying to tell me I couldn't handle this divine purpose that was placed on my life by God. This fast and consecration caused me to get more in God and less into me by not focusing on the "I can't do s", but "I can do all things through Christ which strengthens me."

When growing in God, the enemy wants us to focus on ourselves and our problems. God wants us to focus on what He has given us through His word. We can't do both. It is a matter of changing the mindset from the old to the new. Once this has taken place, we must start applying the Word and watch how our lives will change and how we will be able to affect others lives. Growth and change for the best will take place if you hold on in the process of getting to your purpose and divine destiny.

I can speak from experience now when I go out to teach and preach God's word that it is all about the kingdom work of the Lord. God has a plan for all our lives. That plan is to prosper us spiritual and naturally so we will be able to endure by holding on while growing in the kingdom of the Lord.

~~~

Reflections:

What challenges do you face today?

_____

_____

_____

_____

_____

How will you grow past the challenge (s)?

_____

_____

_____

Who do you know that has faced a similar challenge and had victory?

_____

_____

_____

_____

Scriptures to Ponder:

I can do everything through him who gives me strength. Phillipians 4:13

No weapon that is formed against you shall prosper; and every tongue that shall rise against you in judgment you shall condemn. This is the heritage of the servants of the LORD, and their righteousness is of me, says the LORD.   Isaiah 54:17

David encouraged himself in the Lord. Write a letter of encouragement to yourself.

_____

_____

_____

_____

_____

_____

Chapter 5

Who is He And What Is He to You?

By Sharee Hall

Lady Sharee Hall

Sharee Hall currently resides in the Detroit Metropolitan area, but was born and raised in the western suburbs of Chicago, IL. A God-fearing, virtuous woman, Sharee is married to Henry Hall, Jr., whom she refers to as her "heavenly treasure in the form of an earthen vessel". They celebrate 10 years of marriage. He is the well-abled, anointed and appointed Pastor of the Cedar Christian Church. God has blessed them with two beautiful daughters, Harmony Joi and Harlyn Jade, and for these gifts she is eternally grateful.

She has a passion for wedding and event planning, and she founded her own wedding planning business, "From Yes To I Do". She has operated this successful business for over 14 years. By day, she is a paralegal at a prestigious and prominent law firm, and has been employed there for 12 years.

Cedar Christian Church
1221 E. Lantz
Detroit, MI 48203
313/892-9363Email:
cedarchristianchurchc3@yahoo.com

Who is He and What is He to You?

Ladies, first things first! Can you definitively answer the question that doubles as the title of this chapter? This question has to be more than just rhetorical, and your answer must be sure, strong and serve as the foundation for your ministry. Your answer = your destiny in the Kingdom.

When we talk about a woman's role in the Kingdom, it has everything to do with how you were fashioned and the image in which you were created. Experience has taught me that unless I know who God is, who He is to me, and who I am in Him; I cannot and will not know, understand, nor be able to live out God's plan and purpose for my life. Armed with this knowledge, however, I am a force to be reckoned with; appreciative for who I am in God, and the value that I add to His Kingdom.

"For we are God's own workmanship, recreated in Christ Jesus that we may do those good works which God predestined for us that we should walk in them." Eph 2:10

Women of God, to underscore your appreciation of the fact that you are God's workmanship, let's take a look at three (3) areas that I believe to be a woman's special mission, ordained by God. I call them the "3Ms: Marriage, Motherhood and Ministry."

Marriage

Women are partners of men. *And the Lord God said "it is not good that the man should be alone, I will make him a help meet for him* (Gen 2:18).

Hence, Eve was created from Adam's rib and ordained to be his companion. Man was created first and was physically and emotionally stronger than woman, the weaker vessel (I Pet. 3:7). God's plan for marriage is that man is to be provider, protector, and priest; woman is called to be supportive and submissive. We are subject to our husbands, according to the Word (Eph. 5:22-24, Col. 3:18, Eph. 5:32-33; I Pet. 3:1-6). We cannot compromise. It doesn't matter how much education you have or the degrees behind your name. Your social status, age, and giftedness matter not; your poise, polish and pretty looks will fade. Your husband's social standing may fluctuate or become obsolete; his good looks, intelligence, spiritual condition and attitude still won't change the order of God. Obeying God is what His Word teaches us to do. Yes, I know, you don't mind submitting to Christ, but your husband is another story. Don't get it twisted! This mentality is sin and unfortunately, you are being victimized by worldly thoughts and standards that hold you hostage by the one who convinces us that God's ways are outdated and obsolete.

Let me help you. For a wife to be submissive, she must adopt God's Word. When she does, she is in direct obedience to God; after all, her role is ordained by God. A wife's submission to her husband's authority (which God gave him), is submission to God's authority. It is an attitude, not just an action. Submission begins in the heart and does not make you void of feelings or opinions.

Motherhood

"Train up a child in the way he should go, And when he is old he will not depart from it" Prov. 22:6

One of the most important roles on this earth that God will bless you with is that of motherhood. You have been chosen, called and charged with the task of training up your child. This involves the necessary teaching about God and Jesus; the gifting to them of wise counsel and education; nurturing them according to the Word and in the fear of God. It means communicating with them and being slow to anger and wrath, yet disciplining them, enforcing rules, setting boundaries, and limits because you love them and you know they need them. Yes, it's a lot of work and requires constant attention. However, when you are submissive to the will of the Master, standing on the Word of God, and taking a stand against Satan and his demonic forces, you gain the Spirit's power to deny selfish desires, stand in authority and obedience to Christ, and embrace your role as a mother and greatly appreciate the God-given opportunity.

"Your wife shall be like a fruitful vine, in the very heart of your house, your children like olive plants, all around your table." Psalm 128:3

I love olives!!! Olive plants, like children, grow well in the proper environment. As mothers, you

41

must ensure that this proper environment exists. Training starts at home. You must live right before your children and let them see God in you. You must ensure that they grow and flourish by not only parental influence, but by God's influence. You must lay a foundation of moral standards. Ask God for help with your own faults and failures, and be willing to change. Be motivated by love, not bound to duty with respect to the care of your children. You will be blessed.

"Her *children arise up, and call her blessed; her husband also and he praiseth her.*" Prov. 31:28

Ministry

Our roles in the church have often times been steeped in tradition, and we have become shrinking violets with respect to upholding and obeying God's plan for ministry. Our Heavenly Father has given every believer, not just men, what is necessary to become more like Him, and to achieve all that He has planned for the benefit of the Kingdom. That being said, women are included in this plan and should be able to serve the church in whatever positions they are qualified and sanctified for. It is not necessary for women to be either in a power struggle or in competition with men. In His sovereignty, God's design is a complementary partnership and equal standing for the two before Him, equipped with different roles. Our Father's plan brings order and fulfillment in ministry if followed in obedience. Your role in ministry is birthed out of the gift that the Holy Spirit has bestowed upon you. After all, it is the Holy Spirit that gives gifts as He wills (I Cor. 12:11). Your role in ministry is not birthed out of man's expectation of you, your emulating someone else, nor by adopting some precedent set in ancient stone! Your unique gift does not have to mirror anyone else's either; we have all been given different gifts.

One of the greatest gifts that serve as the foundation for ministry is that the Lord has given us the mind of Christ. The practice of it is our responsibility. Cultivate the mind of Christ within you and guard it against the world's influence. Be not conformed to this world, but be transformed by the renewing of your mind! Do not allow Satan to inject you with his deceit and lies. Refuse to be defined by someone believing themselves to be the authority on how you should function in the Kingdom. Do not allow society or "church folks" to distort what God's plans are, the order He set, and roles he has assigned! Talk to Him.

In ministry, I have come to realize that I will not ever fit the "mold" others have devised for me and I'm too big to fit inside a tiny box! I may not act like they think I should act; think like they think I should think, walk their walk or talk their talk. Guess what? I'm not trying to please them! My role in the Kingdom mirrors the Savior's response when explaining Lazarus' death "...*it is for God's glory so that God's Son may be glorified through it*" (John 11:4). Women of God, look past what others want you to be in order to fulfill who God created you to be.

In order to do this, you must be disciplined by the power of the Holy Spirit like Paul in I Cor. 9. Paul recognized that discipline was necessary to carry out the will of God. Without discipline and accountability, you are not wise nor functioning in the gift that God designed just for you (Prov. 19:20). There is a pre-ordained plan for the purpose of your life and your role in the Kingdom. God is in control and what role you play is up to Him; so, slow your "role"! Seek the will of the Master by spending time in His Word (the revelation of Himself and the plans He has for you). Listen to His voice. Vow to obey Him and surrender to His leading. He will equip you with all you need to bring honor and glory to Him (II Cor. 6:19), and to live out your destiny for His Kingdom. Embrace it, allow the vision of God to break through to your reality in fullness, be excited about who you are in Christ, and who He has pre-destined you to become (I Cor. 6:19).

~~~~

Reflections:

Who is God to you?

_____

_____

_____

_____

Are you effective as a wife, mother, and minister? In which area are you growing?

_____

_____

_____

_____

How can you be a better wife?

_____

_____

_____

_____

How can you be a better mother?

_____

_____

_____

_____

How can you be a better minister?

_____

_____

_____

_____

Scriptures to Ponder:

Her children arise and call her blessed; Her husband

also, and he praises her: Proverbs 31;2

Be imitators of God, therefore, as dearly loved children.

Ephesians 5: 1

-Chapter 6-

Cross The Tracks

By First Lady Angela Bradley

Lady Angela Bradley

Angela Beal **Bradley** is the First Lady of **Valley of Blessings Church** in Hercules, California. She has been happily married to Pastor Bennett Bradley Jr., for 31 years. Lady Bradley's gifts of teaching and leadership have afforded her the opportunity to minister particularly to women and children throughout the country and Canada. She is the Director of "**Know Your Power**" Symposium designed to equip and empower women in all aspects of life. She is also the Founder and Executive Director of **Nia Imani Academy** a Tutorial/Performing Arts program designed to promote the scholastic achievement of all children, particularly African American males. Lady Bradley enjoys being a mother of three children and one granddaughter. She has a deep abiding love for the Lord, and a mind to tenaciously work to build up God's Kingdom.

Valley of Blessings Church Nia Imani Academy 111 Civic Dr. 5570 Olinda Rd. Hercules, CA 94547 El Sobrante, CA 94803 (510) 799-4448 www.niaimaniacademy.com

CROSS THE TRACKS

"Lie down B_ _ _ _ before I kill you! If you don't shut up I'll tie you down and let the train run over you!" Those words echoed through my mind and pierced my soul. I was penned against a set of railroads tracks less than a mile away from home...yet it felt like a thousand. This wasn't the first time I was violated, but somehow, some way I promised myself if I survived, this would be the last!

I was only fourteen years old and he was my first "*boyfriend.*" I often ask myself, " Why did I feel so compelled to have a boyfriend?" I wasn't searching for love from my father because he was there and an excellent provider. I knew he loved me; we had a very special bond. What was I searching for? Why did I allow someone to abuse me this way?

After this troubled, angry young man tortured me, I walked home torn to pieces. When I arrived, the house was empty. I needed help and no one was there. My parents had gone to visit my oldest sister for the evening. It couldn't have been very late, but midnight and a deep darkness covered my soul. I knew I had to tell somebody. I felt guilty because I had disobeyed my father's wishes. He told me on several occasions not to interact with boys from a certain area of town but...I was hardheaded. Was this my punishment? I wrestled within. Should I tell someone or conceal it and bare the pain again. After all, I contributed to this, didn't I? "No!" "No" another voice cried. Even though I disobeyed, I didn't deserve to be treated like this. That night I broke out of the cells of abuse.

I dialed my sister's number. "Hello... hello... hello, who's there?" Silence filled the air. Finally I blurted out, "…. I just got raped" Right then I was free! My abuser could no longer hold me captive because I opened my mouth and told somebody! I was rushed to the police station where I was examined and interrogated. Who was he? Did I know him? Had I consented to have sex at any point?

After hours of questioning they did N-O-T-H-I-N-G. Absolutely nothing!

A day later he had the audacity to call, acting as if nothing happened. But when he heard my voice he knew something had changed. I informed him that I filed a police report, so I think that bit of information scared him to a certain extent. But the tone in my voice let him know not to come near me again.

Though I learned the hard way, I acquired some valuable life lessons. First of all, disobedience opens a door and allows the enemy to trespass against your mind, body and soul. I heard my father's voice but I failed to heed. I thought it was natural to want a boyfriend. I was maturing so I thought I could handle it. The point is, young women fail to realize the sacredness of their bodies. There's a time and season for everything. Intimate relationships are to be within marriage "Don't wake my love till he pleases" (Song of Solomon). We get ourselves into a lot of unproductive relationships that cause years and sometimes generations of pain! So let us practice obedience in every area of our lives, especially listening to our elders. More importantly listen to your heavenly Father's voice and the Word of God. You will save yourself a lot of heartache.

The second lesson I learned was to set boundaries. Men (and people in general) don't do anymore than you allow them to do. Never again would anyone have that much control over my mind or body. Five years after that ordeal, I got saved and gave myself to the Lord. I yielded my body as a temple for the Holy Ghost to dwell. A few years later, I got married and although I was saved, I still had to be delivered and healed from that traumatic event. Certain things would trigger the memories. In many ways some affected my personality and relationship with my husband. It took years to heal.

I also learned we overcome by our testimony. I don't share this part of my life often but it liberates me more each time I do so. The first time I shared it, someone advised me not to be so transparent. I guess I was supposed to keep it to myself and not help others become free. No, I will not allow the devil to have the upper hand.

Women often remain captives because we don't tell our stories.

I've come to understand that we are to share our lives so others might overcome. For too long we have kept "secrets". Thousands have gone to their graves with secrets, others have become the walking dead burying the burden in their hearts. We try to wash, or even eat it away, to anesthetize the pain. Some use drugs, alcohol, or sex. Or we simply erect a wall to protect ourselves and promise that we won't let anyone hurt us like that again. But the more we do that, we stop the healing process and even hinder the overflow of blessings from ourselves to others. We must open up and *be real*.

Learning to forgive and move forward was a major challenge. But I realized that in order not to develop a "*victim*" mentality, I had to let it go. I had to forgive that young man and myself because I did not want to be imprisoned to unforgiveness, resentment and hatred for the rest of my life.

I was searching for love and to fill a void that was reserved only for God. I had to learn to love myself, to treasure who I was in Christ so I wouldn't become a victim of self hate. Ladies we must learn what true love is...it casts out all fear!

It is God's will that we be free, free indeed. Sisters write, tell your story. Publish it! Don't allow the enemy to make his forlorn abode.

Depart from that abusive, demoralizing relationship. No matter who you are, you deserve better. God declared, *"I have come that you might have life and that you might have it more abundantly."* It's up to you. You have the power!

Set yourself free! As the famous Shakespeare quote declares, "To thine own self be true." Too many of you are saying that you're "waiting on God" but sometimes the real truth is...God is waiting on you to trust and believe in Him. Don't be abused, co-dependent or bound by tradition or even religion. If you do you will be allowing the "in-a-me" (enemy) to hold you captive and tie you down on the railroad tracks without anything attaching you. The enemy will rape you of the very essence of life, but don't allow him to do so.

Break out of the cell of abuse. Be free to walk in your rightful position---cross the tracks to freedom in Christ!

~~~~

Reflections:

Do you have any secrets that you wouldn't want anyone else to know? Name a traumatic event in your past?

_____

_____

_____

_____

_____

_____

Have you been healed? Have you forgiven the offender and yourself?

_____

_____

_____

_____

Scriptures to Ponder:

They overcame him by the blood of the Lamb and by the word of their testimony; they did not love their lives so much as to shrink from death.
Revelation 12:11 (NIV)

And be ye kind one to another, tenderhearted, forgiving one another, even as God for Christ's sake hath forgiven you. Ephesians 4:32

Write your testimony. Tell your story so that someone else can be healed.

_____

_____

_____

_____

_____

_____

_____

_____

_____

- Chapter 7 -

Shut My Mouth

By Elder Joceline Bronson

Elder Joceline Bronson

Elder Joceline Bronson, a native of Detroit, MI. is the wife of Prentice
Bronson for 22 years, and mother of 5 children;
Emory 29, Aries 28, Westley 25, Will 22, and
Bianca 20, and a doting grandmother of 3,
Anthony, Westley and Javon.

Joceline is the Co-pastor of Greater Works Family
Ministries. She is also the Co-publisher of Destiny
House Publishing, LLC.

Joceline has a heart for wounded women. Her
passion is that all women are healed, delivered
and set free. She is also the author of "Barren,
Yet Pregnant With Promise." Joceline's prayer is
that every woman comes into the fullness and
freedom of who God called her to be.

Greater Works Family Ministries
19136 Joy Road
Detroit, MI 48228 313.836.GWFM (4936)
www.gwfmchurch.org
email:jbronson@gwfmchurch.org

"Shut My Mouth"

I was born prematurely. My mother was 7 months pregnant when she delivered me. One of the nurses said, "Wow, she's so little you can put her in your pocket!" My grandfather said that one of my parents stated, "That little ugly thing is not my baby, my baby is one of those big babies over there."

My story began back about 48 years ago, that is when the devil first tried to shut my mouth. I was born in October 1963 to Mr. and Mrs. Joe C McCloud, a beautiful, bouncing, baby girl, named, Jo Celine McCloud, after my father. This is the dream of every mother and father, right?

Well let me re-track my words. This is what I was told: I was not bouncing or beautiful, no not at all. I was just a little over 2 lbs in weight. I was just a little ugly fragile thing.

I was born addicted to heroin; I needed to go in the incubator for months to grow, for my lungs to develop and to be weaned off the drugs. My mother and father both were on drugs at the time of my conception. My father was a drug user, dealer and pimp. My mother was a drug user and prostitute. Their drugs of choice in that time and era were cocaine and heroin. Their drug use caused a lot of complications in my birth. The doctors did not think I was going to make it. I had a hernia on my stomach. I had the shakes, low birth weight, stigmatism in my eyes, and the list goes on.

But I was alive.

That alone makes me want to shout! And still to this day the thought brings tears to my eyes. God is worthy of the praise because I'm alive. Praise The Lord! The devil did not silence me nor did he take my testimony and did not shut my mouth! All Glory belongs to God! I should not be here.

In the 60's medical science was neither as developed nor as advanced as it is now. But God was and is. The Bible says He is the same yesterday, today and forever more. So the same miracles He performs today with medical science, he performed with me back then without the advancement of it. Hallelujah! He said, "My daughter you were predestined before the foundation of the world, and I knew you in your mother's drug infested womb!"

"Before I formed thee in the belly I knew thee; and before thou camest forth out of the womb I sanctified thee, and I ordained thee a prophet unto the nations." Jeremiah 1:5

I was raised by my grandfather and grandmother who took me home from the hospital when it was time for my release from Detroit Metropolitan Hospital. From that moment of my birth and upon my arrival at my grandparents, the devil wanted to silence me, even as a little girl. He wanted to stop my mother's seed.

The following scripture is why, the devil is upset with me, you and every other women. This is why he wants to shut your mouth. Genesis 3:15 " And I will put enmity between you and the woman and between your seed and her Seed; He shall bruise your head..."

The devil hates woman because she is the bearer of the seed. So because of that he wants to plant other seeds in women to destroy her destiny and her seed. He wants to deceive us, and never let us find out who we are in Christ. The devil wants to do a repeat of what he did to Eve in the garden, which is beguile you and steal your promise.

As I began to grow from a premature baby to a little girl, the devil planted ungodly seeds in me. He planted the idea that I was ugly. I was dark and unwanted; the incubator burned me. I had seeds of self pity and rejection. So many more seeds of death were planted. These seeds were planted from this sad unbelievably true story that you just read. This story was being told to me over and over again over the years. Each time, I heard it, the wound's scab was scraped off and the healing process had to start over. Each account of this story I got from my relatives. Each account was different .No account was good or better than the other. They were all about defeat.

I heard that one time my mother needed drug money and she sold me for $2.00 dollars. My grandfather said I was in pawn for $2.00 he had to pay to get me out of pawn. I have to praise God every time I see how the devil tried to take me out. But God said not so! What a mighty God we serve! Even though no account was exactly the same they all had a common denominator and that was, I was born premature, addicted to drugs, and unwanted by my mother and father. The spirit of rejection was already imparted in me from birth and now it began to manifest and cause me to feel useless, unloved and it began to silence me.

The devil wanted to destroy me. He wanted me to keep hearing different versions of this story as a little girl. So every time I heard this story and another version of this story seeds of rejection would be replanted over and over. This was creating a sinful mess. I never shared my pain, my hurt with family. I never told them to stop telling me the story that I had heard a million times. I never told them this makes me feel this way. I learned how to hold it in and keep quiet and how to hurt and hide. I learned how to be invisible.

The devil began silencing me at an early age. It was not enough that he tried to kill me at birth but he had to go for the jugular and put the nail in the coffin, and try to destroy my mind, body, spirit. While living with my grandparents, my uncle molested me. I was between four and five years old. That planted seeds of lust, unforgiveness and many other seeds of defeat. The molestation gave me a fear of men; yet I desired them through lust. The lust I thought was love caused a downward spiral. I went into my adolescence, then adult life I began to look for love in men that showed hate and abuse. And that is what I married. It caused me to shut up and go into hiding. It became a normal part of life for me to just hide my pain and my past. The devil had made headway.

But God had a different plan for my life. He sent someone to minister Christ to me 24 years ago and I got saved. He said to me, *"Before **I** formed thee in the belly I knew thee; and before thou camest forth out of the womb I sanctified thee, and I ordained thee a prophet unto the nations."* Jeremiah 1:5

I was saved but not delivered. I was a saved hot mess. I thought because of salvation, all the pain of my past would instantly disappear. But I needed to be delivered. God began to deliver me from the hurt, the un-forgiveness, the abuse, the lust, the self pity, the rejection, and from the demons of my past. I would get delivered and then go back into hiding, because my mind was not free. Old things were not passed away and I was not new; I was just in hiding. I was married in an abusive relationship while preaching the gospel. I was silent even though I was preaching the Word out loud. That was the trick of the devil. *She calls herself free but I got her mind in bondage and she is still hiding while preaching.* You may think of a women preaching as liberty and freedom. If she is ministering the word then she must be free, *He who the son sets free is free indeed.* No, I was laying hands on Sunday, praying for people and they were getting delivered. On Monday I was laying in the bed in pain hiding and crying from hurt from emotional and mental abuse. But God used my leaders to inform me that I needed to become free and that I needed to see myself as God sees me. The rejection is still who I think I am. But that is not who God says I am, and that began the real process of my deliverance and opening my

65

mouth. I knew my mouth was shut up before salvation but the devil had me deceived while in salvation that I was ok. *"HOW COULD I BE HIDING? I'm a minister"* It was all a lie from the devil. I was bound.

My testimony is so powerful to me that God showed Himself mightily on my behalf and spared my life for His Glory. This was so I can share my story so other women will open their mouths and not let the devil steal their destiny or their testimony. Finally, I got it ! It was the best time in my life. I had just become debt-free. I had decided, " It is me and you Jesus." For God I live for God I die. REALLY! I decided he could not shut me up. It's on now devil! I finally came out of hiding. God is good. I'm no longer in the abusive relationship, I am ready to go forth in ministry; no holds barred. The Lord gave me a new ministry called "No Longer Shattered". I was so excited about this. I kept thinking "Send me, Lord, I will go. I will not shut my mouth." This season of my life was a season of excitement! I was basking in the midst of my new found freedom from bondage, a new position, an elevation in ministry, new business with my new business partner. My children were all gone and grown. I thought, "Could it get any better than this? I am finally free and I will not let the devil shut me up!" While basking in His presence seeing His Glory manifested and His goodness, I was diagnosed with stage 3 Ovarian Cancer.

Why me? Haven't I suffered enough? I struggled. But not like before. Cancer shut my mouth. But it was quickly reopened with praise. God did this thing so quick. I don't know what happened. God did not allow me to stay in my pity party. I was diagnosed, had an operation, they got *all* the cancer. They took out the tumor and I am currently in chemo for any residue. My church family and pastors supported me through the entire ordeal. I have to give God all the praise. This last blow from devil was supposed to be my destiny. I heard this the day I was diagnosed. I was supposed to go and resign from ministry and go into hiding. I was to never launch, "No Longer Shattered." I was to pull away from everything and everybody and go into hiding and die. The devil tried to shut my mouth this last time. It did not work! I proclaimed that I shall live and not die and declare the works of the Lord!

Women of God, no matter what your circumstance or trial, no matter your past or your present, don't ever let the devil shut your mouth. Because you win!

~~~~

Reflections:

How is the enemy trying to close your mouth?

_____

_____

_____

_____

Are you presently dealing with the spirit of rejection in your life? If so, where is it coming from? How will you overcome it?

_____

_____

_____

_____

_____

_____

_____

_____

_____

_____

_____

_____

Scriptures to Ponder:

I, the LORD, have called you in righteousness; I will take hold of your hand. I will keep you and will make you to be a covenant for the people and a light for the Gentiles. Isaiah 42:6.

All that the Father gives me will come to me, and whoever comes to me I will never cast out.   John 6:37

Write a list indicating the times in your life that you felt rejected. Then next to each one write a scripture of victory and comfort.

_____

_____

_____

_____

_____

_____

_____

_____

- Chapter 8 -

On My Knees

Claudia Thomas

Pastor Claudia Thomas

Pastor Claudia is the wife of Lepoleon Thomas, the mother of 3 great sons (Leon, David and Daniel) and 1 awesome daughter, (Lavonne), and the beaming grandmother of 4 (Bryan, Aaron, Samiya, and Leah).

Claudia is an entrepreneur, her business is CJ Classique, where she sells designer handbags and jewelry.

Claudia is an intercessor and Bible teacher at Cedar Christian Church. Pastor Claudia is commissioned to a life of prayer.

Cedar Christian Church
1221 E. Lantz
Detroit, MI 48203
313/892-9363
Email: cedarchristianchurchc3@yahoo.com

On My Knees

It happened one late Saturday night at 11:58p.m. You know if you are a church going person, that means you are preparing for church on the next day. That is exactly what I was doing; preparing and getting outfits together for Sunday service.

I was walking to get into bed after making all my preparations. As I walked into the bedroom, the Holy Spirit speaks to me. The Holy Spirit reminds me of something. He says, "Remember the Adversary took your older brother's life early. He was murdered at the age of 35. I was having a conversation with the Lord, and said "Yes I remember". Then he said "He (the adversary) wants to take your son, David's life."

As He, the Holy Spirit says this to me, I fell on my knees by my bedside and I said, "Lord don't take my son, Lord, don't take my son's life. Please save his life. Don't let him die."

At that moment, the phone rang.

My husband answered the phone. It is Beaumont Hospital on the phone. They asked, "Are you the parent of David Thomas?" "Yes" he responded." The person on the other line continued, "David has been in a bad accident. We don't expect him to live. We will put him on life support until you get here."

We got dressed and ran to the hospital. On the way to the hospital, my husband and I began to take authority over the spirit of death. I started calling and waking people up to tell them the situation and to ask that they pray for David. When we arrived at the hospital, they would not let us see him. One of the nurses came out and talked with us. She asked if we wanted a priest to come pray with us. She showed us the chapel. We replied, "No, we are the priests." We went into the family waiting room.

The nurse brought us David's belongings, cell phone and his wallet. As I picked up his items, my heart dropped. I knew this situation was serious.

I went out into hallway to call my oldest son, Leon. When I returned into the waiting room, I saw my husband and younger son, Daniel just crying. The doctor had just left them, giving them more bad news.

They said David's accident was traumatic. He was not wearing a seat belt and had went through the windshield of the car that he was driving. The car went off the road and hit a house. He has grand mal seizures and had lost a lot a blood and wasn't going to make it. And if he did survive, he would be a vegetable; not being able to walk or talk.

We sat in the waiting room unsure of how to handle all of this information. But I thank God for the prayers of the righteous. About 20 minutes later the doctor came back out and said that they were going to take him into surgery to at least sew up his face. He was cut from the top of his forehead all the way to his ear.

By this time a large portion of our family had arrived to the hospital. The surgery took at least 4 hours and the doctor came back to the waiting room. He said they sewed up one side of his face. However, his left lung had also collapsed. They also had to cut from the lung to his stomach because he had so much fluid that had built up. The surgeon told us that his face was fractured in his forehead, his cheek bone and his lower face area. He said we just sewed him up to stop the bleeding. He eye was also cut and they are not sure if he would see out of it if by any slight chance he did live. Doctors said that the next several hours would tell the story if he lives.

Thank God for answering prayers. It was about 6am on Sunday. My family went home to pray and go to the church. My husband, his brother, and I stayed at the hospital. It was during that morning in the waiting room, that I begin to talk to God.

I sat in the waiting room and I couldn't believe what had happened. I was in shock. I couldn't believe that the Devil was trying to take my son's life. Sometimes you pray to God, and there are times in your life that you understand that every prayer you have ever prayed, every word you have ever spoken over the life of your children: you need to draw on that. You need a miracle turn your situation around.

I waited in that waiting room. I was the only person there at the time. I talked out loud to the Father. I said, "God I know my David is in heaven with you; but you tell him that his mother said, he can't stay up in heaven with you. HE HAS GOT TO COME BACK. I' m not letting him go."

It took every fiber of my being to speak in the authority that God had given me to walk. I understood my position as a mother, that God had given me power to speak over my children and call to be what God wanted them to be. I understood my place in God.
David remained in a coma. On the third day, he woke up. His medical condition was changed from critical to stable. He continued to stay in intensive care for 23 more days.

Each day, God performed another miracle, each day of those 35 days. God did something, to let us know that we he was with us. His body was so swollen, It was hard to tell who he was. When he first came out of the coma, on the third day, his eyes were so swollen he could barely see.

When David opened his eyes, he knew me. They didn't think he would know anybody. I thought he was going to be glad to see me and express that. But, he didn't say that. I was totally shocked by the very first words that came out of his mouth.

Looking at him talk to me, I began to cry. This was my son who the doctor had said would die. He is still alive, he knows who I am and he is talking to me!

Then I realized what he was saying to me. He said, "Ma, why did you ask me to come back? I wanted to stay; I wanted to stay where I was."

God had used my son to let me know that he had heard my prayers; our prayers. And that he had answered.

I understand that God had placed my children in my hands to care for, take care, and to pray for them until they get where God wants them to be. This is my place as a woman. I consider this a ministry and I take it seriously.

It is my place as a mother, a woman of God, to lead my children to God: to stand in the gap for them until they find God for themselves. And to never give up.

My David came through every challenge of the enemy. He learned how to walk, talk, and to eat again.

At one point because of his closed head injury, he had problems with his mind. My God has bought him through it all and he no longer has that problem. David is an intelligent young man, currently working on his Bachelors of Science Degree.

Knowing my place, as a mother, and a woman of God, helped save my son's life. God is serious about our place as women. Are you?

Reflections:

How would you rate your prayer life? What prayer requests do you have before the Lord?

_____

_____

_____

_____

_____

What prayers has God answered most recently?

_____

_____

_____

_____

Scriptures to Ponder:

Do not fret or have any anxiety about anything, but in every circumstance and in everything, by prayer and petition (definite requests), with thanksgiving, continue to

*make your wants known to God. Philippians 4: 6
(AMP)*

*The Lord has heard my supplication; the Lord receives
my prayer. Psalm 6: 9 (NKJV)*

Write a prayer to the Lord and His response to you.

_____

_____

_____

_____

_____

_____

_____

_____

_____

_____

_____

_____

_____

Chapter 9

A Woman's Call

By Pastor Tonya Dillard

Pastor Tonya Dillard

Pastor Tonya is called for such a time as this by GOD to minister the gospel of Jesus Christ with simplicity and power to those that are in need of healing and breakthrough. She is a graduate of Logos Ministerial Institute and currently pastors alongside her husband, Pastor Michael Dillard at Chosen Generation Christian Center and is the proud mother of two daughters.

Chosen Generation Christian Center

1045 Dixie Highway

Chicago Heights, IL 60466

A Woman's Call

A woman's place in ministry is always where God has specifically called her and in whatever way God has prepared her and shown himself strong in her life and instructed her.

Your anointing may be in the area of an intercessor, church administrator, praise and worship leader or altar worker. Every woman is not called to minister behind the pulpit. Every woman must absolutely know that the Lord called her and to whom he called her to reach. Listen to the spirit of God and be obedient to his instruction.

I am convinced that too many women in ministry today are mimicking others instead of seeking God for direction for their own lives. Women of God, it is up to you to find out by praying, fasting and asking God to show you what area of ministry he wants you in.

One of my favorite books in the Bible is the story about Esther. Esther, like most of you did not ask for her call; she was summoned. Esther was then groomed and prepared for her calling. This is a very critical point that has generally been missed in the kingdom. Her appointment as queen was just the beginning of her responsibilities and ultimate purpose for her position. She was not placed in the coveted position of queen for her own enjoyment and comfort. This leadership position came with a price.

You must stay focused on why you are where God called. You are in the position you are in to reach souls because it's not only about you!

Esther was a praying woman, which is a requirement for any call in ministry. I often wondered what would have happened if Esther tried to go in front of the king without a prayer life; without the preparation, without favor and in her own strength?

Humility is birthed through prayer and consecration. Esther's combination of wisdom and prayer produced a power and influence that set the decree of the Lord. When women of God learn to operate in wisdom and power in her assigned place, she will have a level of influence and power unprecedented. What I like about Esther is she had so much favor that she broke the law and lived! Esther has so much favor that the king offered her half of his kingdom. Esther had so much favor she set the decree without being King!

God is a family man; the whole church began as a family and is going to end with a family. It is the call of the woman of the house to ensure that her family is taken care of. She builds the house and creates an environment that is God-fearing and loving. Building up the house refers to making sure everything, everyone and every person within the house is in proper alignment. I believe the main responsibility of the woman is to make sure she is ministering to her whole family. You cannot do anything great in the kingdom of God, if your house is neglected. Do not give place to the devil in your house, in your marriage and in your children. I know too many women who have not accepted their responsibilities for their families and consequently their families are paying the price.

I am not saying that your family should or will be perfect. Raising children will have its ups and downs. You must remember that, because of your spiritual position, the devil wants to embarrass and destroy you. The devil will always try to attack you through your weakest link which is often your children and sometimes your spouse. Remember patience is a virtue and a necessary ingredient in both ministry and marriage. Without patience, you will blow up, give up and fail to reach God's plan for your life.

The Bible says that it is through faith and patience that we inherit the promises. It will be your patience that will see you through your marriage and the ups and downs of ministry. The fear of the Lord is reverential respect and awe of God. I believe this is one of the key elements that is missing in our homes, marriages and ministries.

There is so much more to say about the woman's place. Ask yourself this, am I a woman that is still full of issues? Eve had food issues, Potipher's wife and Delilah had trouble with men, Lot's wife and Michal couldn't let go of their past. We know that Sapphira could not let go of her money and

Jezebel could not let go of anything and wanted to run everything.

You may be one of the Naomi's, giving impartations or the Ruth going out of your way to receive one. Either way, it requires you to come out of your comfort zone and totally commit your body, soul and spirit to God and his purpose for your life. Find out what you are called to do.

~~~~

Reflections:

What do you feel called to do?

_____

_____

_____

_____

What are your gifts, talents, and abilities? Are you using them to give God glory?

_____

_____

_____

_____

_____

What is your responsibility to your family? Are you balanced or working towards balance?

_____

_____

_____

How can you be a better example to your family? What area can you improve in?

_____

_____

_____

_____

_____

Scriptures to Ponder:

Likewise, teach the older women to be reverent in the way they live, not to be slanderers or addicted to much wine, but to teach what is good. Titus 2:3 NIV

Neglect not the gift that is in thee, which was given thee by prophecy, with the laying on of the hands of the presbytery. II Timothy 4:14

Chapter 10

A Woman's Position is Not Her Place

By Pastor Michelle Morris

Pastor Michelle Morris

Pastor Michelle is a woman of God who has made the decision to be lead and directed by the Lord. She is the adoring wife of Prophet James Stapleton-Morris.

In June 2010, God blessed them with a Ministry where she Co-Pastors with her husband, Perfecting the Saints Spirit Led Ministries, in Oakland, CA. She is also the blessed mother of four wonderful children, Hashina, Miya, Henry and Micah. They all serve with her in the ministry.

She is greatly loved, respected and supported by her family and friends.

Perfecting The Saints Spirit-Led Ministries

P.O. Box 4

Fremont, CA 94537

A Woman's Position is Not Her Place

When I was asked to have a thought on this subject, it took me a while to know exactly how I would express my opinion, but I first had to ask myself what really is the Kingdom of God? What does this really mean? Hearing so many preachers and messages, I was excited to know that the Kingdom of God would come and I would be with God forever. Not realizing that the kingdom of God is already here. Well after I looked I understood that the Kingdom of God is simple. It is a spiritual kingdom where God rules.

Living in this natural world where the people rule, we call it a Democracy. It is a form of government in which all eligible people have an equal say in the decisions that affect their lives. Who set up this government, who is eligible? It seems to have complicated many lives. That's funny, so many things that we experience today, we have not had an equal say in. This democracy has been an unfair and unjust system. Ruled parties, by emotions and opinions, ruled by hate and prejudices and without upholding and respecting the rulership greater than what we see "God." God is hard to find in this government called Democracy. We are known for being one nation under God, but even that now has been taken out.

As many struggle with the unfairness, we are reminded of how all things came about and it is there, that we find assurance and comfort. We know that we are not of this world and so we are ruled by a God that sits high (Isaiah 66:1-2) and is greater than anything that we can experience here on earth.

I am reminded of the scripture in Genesis 1:1, in the beginning *God* created the heaven and the earth and everything that's in it. Not only did God create the world, but God created woman. This lets me know that God had a plan for women not only in the world but in the Kingdom of God. Woman was created with man; she was taken from the rib of man. There was not a suitable helpmeet for Adam. Here we come, we were to be fruitful and multiply replenish the earth and subdue it and have dominion over everything that moves upon the earth. How is that significant to the kingdom of God? It was his rulership that should have been obeyed because God was the authority and woman had a place on the earth in God's kingdom. God's kingdom is established here on the earth and the kingdom is within you. Luke 17:21.

Since we have established what the Kingdom of God is and where it is, realize that women have had many roles and held many positions. The one thing that I want to make plain is the place we have in the Kingdom is to know where we should be and who placed us there. We were created to help and we were placed in a capacity to replenish to bear fruit and multiply.   What are you doing with the place you have been given? Do you consider your place to be less valuable because you are not first? Do you consider yourself least?

1 Corinthians the 12th Chapter is a beautiful expression of Gods Rulership and what he designed and desired. The 18th verse in the NIV says, "But in fact, God has placed the parts in the body, every one of them, as he wanted them to be." Your position does not determine your place.

We as flesh place value on position. Because you are a housewife and are happy serving your family is no less of a position than being a Pastor over a church. Being a prayer warrior is no less or more valuable than being an usher. Establish that Gods Kingdom is the greatest Kingdom, demonstrated by our confession, our belief and ultimately our lifestyle. Because you are the eye, it does not give you more value. You just simply should do your part and see. Give light to the entire body, allow the Spirit of God to illuminate the body and be careful not to be drawn away by your ability to see that you do not lead the entire body into the wrong place. Women in the Kingdom should function as they have been instructed by the Lord. You hear the old saying, "Stay in your lane" do you and be the best that you can be?

So many people are trying to define where the role and place of women should be. We are okay in one place but not in another. Depending on your denomination it can be a definition of how you are placed and received in the church, but that is not necessarily how you are viewed from the Kingdom's standpoint. Based on this scripture it says, "God!" Since its God then man can't define a woman's place in the Kingdom because he is not the originator and created nothing outside of what God allowed him to handle in the earth. Women, we must know the voice of God and be able to know where he has placed you to serve him. He placed us as it pleased him. Don't allow your position to make you believe that you are more or less valuable, rather recognize your value is being in your place as it pleases the Lord.

~~~~~~

Reflections:

What position do you hold in your church?
On your job? In your community?

_____

_____

_____

_____

_____

Do you know your place in God's kingdom? If so,
What is your place?

_____

_____

_____

Do you struggle with your self-image? Do you know
your place in God?

_____

_____

Scriptures to Ponder:

There is no longer Jew or Greek, there is no longer
slave or free, there is no longer male and female; for all of
you are one in Christ Jesus. Galatians 3:28

Then Mary said, 'Here am I, the servant
of the Lord; let it be with me according to
your word. (Luke 1:38)

Write a praise to the Lord.

_____

_____

_____

_____

_____

_____

_____

_____

_____

_____

_____

Chapter 11
Walking In Purpose
By Prophetess Cynthia McKinney

Prophetess Cynthia McKinney

Prophetess Cynthia McKinney, co-pastor of Greater Works Deliverance Ministries in Collierville, TN works in unison with her husband in ministry. It is her desire to see women walking in their destiny according to the plan of God. She serves as leader of the "Women of Virtue" Women's Ministry and "Blossoming Virtuously" Purity class for teens. She is blessed to be married to Apostle Joseph McKinney and the mother of six beautiful children.

Greater Works Deliverance Ministries

449 Hwy 72 W., Collierville, TN 38017

(901) 853-6445

Walking in Purpose

I am so humbled to have this opportunity to share with you my view on a woman's place in the kingdom. I believe it is the will of God that you recognize and understand the purpose and plan that he desires to transpire in your life. For some of us we have struggled with the question, does God use women for kingdom purpose? We've allowed fear and the spirit of tradition to lock us out from the true intent of God for our lives. **When the Lord formed you he did not forget to attach purpose within you.**

There is kingdom purpose inside of you and God will release the strength you need to birth it through. We've been told by some that our place in the kingdom is to keep quiet, submit and pray. There is a time and place for that.   Proverbs 4:7 *Wisdom is the principal thing; therefore get wisdom: and with all thy getting get understanding*. Because of the lack of understanding, we've allowed this weight to be dropped in our spirits. We believe that we as women are not called by God to go forth in the work of the Lord; we are not to be heard. It is my belief that in this season the Lord's desire is to loose you from the chains of tradition, which informs us how we should look, act, and sound as women in the house of God. When you walk in tradition, which according to Webster's dictionary is *a continuing pattern of culture beliefs or practices; the handing down of statements, customs, or beliefs from generation to generation,* you become hindered from God's true plan for your life. We are walking in the shadows of those who created plans without clear understanding from the word of God.

For God so loved the world, that he gave his only begotten son, that whosoever believeth in him should not perish, but have everlasting life (John 3:16). The Word of the Lord and his kingdom work is not for a select group of people but he gave his life for male and female, all shapes and sizes. There is a unique character in all of us and we are blessed when we walk in it.

When you study the scripture, you will learn of so many powerful women God chose to use. He placed assignments in their hands and graced them to carry it through. When the Lord knows he can trust you, he will use you to carry out great assignments for the building of his kingdom. *Jesus Christ is the same yesterday, and today, and forever* (Hebrew 13:8). If the Lord was using women back then why wouldn't he use us now? The word says he doesn't change. *For I am the Lord, I change not* (Malachi 3:6). He gave us many great examples to follow as women doing kingdom work. In Judges the fourth chapter, the Lord used Deborah, who was a prophetess and a judge to speak to Barak causing him to go into a battle that he won and it avenged the Jews. We also have the woman at the well in Samaria, though her lifestyle was different and not of God.

After the Lord spent time with her, he brought her to deliverance. Now after the Lord forgave her of her sins he then used her to go and witness. We are sometimes guilty of allowing people to keep us in our past and sometimes we are our own enemy, refusing to forgive ourselves of our past history. The Lord washed you so he can use you for his glory.

There were often times in the scripture when the Lord used women to stop the plan of the enemy. I'm a big reader of the book of Esther and I teach my "Blossoming Virtuously" purity class from this book. For me, I've receive many different revelations from the Lord reading this book. Esther had such wisdom and strength. Esther didn't come from a place of royalty and she even encountered some hurt in her life. She wasn't blessed to be raised by her parents; death had taken them leaving her to be raised by a family member named Mordecai. Life offered her some challenges but it didn't detour her from walking in her purpose.

Women of God, sometimes life will leave you feeling empty, unworthy and defeated but that does not change the plan of God for your life. *For I know the thoughts that I think toward you, saith the Lord, thoughts of peace, and not of evil, to give you an expected end* (Jeremiah 29:11). The Lord knew how your end would turn out when you were just at the beginning. The Lord used Esther because there was destruction coming to her people and someone had to be in position to intercept the plan of Satan. Esther lined up with the plan of God and in doing so the lives of the Jews were saved and promotions were given. It only took one woman walking in obedience to God.

Esther's true purpose was fulfilled because she had the wisdom to position herself on her knees. Women of God, your true kingdom purpose will be birthed when you position yourself in the face of God. What will the Lord use you to do for him when you position yourself in prayer before him? Prayer and fasting will not only get you to your kingdom purpose but it will allow wisdom to connect to you. Esther never spoke out of turn she was in tune to God, causing her to speak in a time when the king would receive her. When there is true relationship with the Lord, your words will be effective because they will line up with the timing of God.

We spend most of our time pondering and trying to sort between what the Lord is saying in comparison to what others are saying concerning us. *Trust in the Lord with all thine heart; and lean not unto thine own understanding. In all thy ways acknowledge him, and he shall direct thy paths* (Proverbs 3:5,6). We must learn to trust God's plan for our lives.

I encourage you to build a solid relationship with the Lord. Create an altar of prayer, praise and worship in your private time with God. Don't allow the cares of life to detour you from your true purpose. It is important to keep your mind and heart clear and free from bondage. *Thou wilt keep him in perfect peace, whose mind is stayed on thee: because he trusteth in thee* (Isaiah 26:3). We've allowed things and the challenges of life to detour us from our kingdom purpose.

It's time for you to seek the Lord for your kingdom purpose and when you find it, walk in it. Voids will be filled in our life when we walk in the plan of God. What did God call you to do? What is his purpose for your life? Who are you assigned to help? What is your place in the kingdom? Well, you will soon find the answers to these questions when you free up time in your busy day to seek after God. *O God, thou art God; early will I seek thee* (Psalm 63:1). Yield yourself to fasting and prayer, the Lord is already there and he's waiting on you.

 Position yourself to walk in your divine kingdom purpose, become thirsty for God and trust that he has the master plan.

~~~~

Reflections:

Have you forgiven yourself of past sins?

_____

_____

How has God used you to help others in the past?

_____

_____

_____

How is the Lord using you to help others currently?

_____

_____

_____

Why do you think God created you?

_____

_____

_____

Scriptures to Ponder:

For I have come down from heaven not to do My own will and purpose but to do the will and purpose of Him Who sent Me.   John 6: 38 (AMP)

Many plans are in a man's mind, but it is the Lord's purpose for him that will stand. Proverbs 19: 21 (AMP)

I will cry to God Most High, Who performs on my behalf and rewards me [Who brings to pass His purposes for me and surely completes them]!   Psalm 57: 2

Write out your purpose statement:

_____

_____

_____

_____

_____

Chapter 12

Restoration of God's Vessels

By Torrona Tillman

Prophetess Torrona Tillman

Torrona F Tillman is a native of Chicago, IL and the
seventh of eight children. She gave her life to the
Lord at an early age and joyfully continues on her
destiny journey for His Glory. Torrona is married to
her best friend and life partner, Apostle Larry Tillman,
senior pastor and teacher of New Destiny Christian
Center in Merrillville, IN. They are the honored and
blessed parents of Lauren Renee' and Larry Jr., both
attending high school and assisting in ministry.
Prophetess Tillman is a woman of God with a calling
for spiritual activation and restoration in the body of
Christ. She declares the Word of the Lord with a
strong and passionate voice without compromise to
bring about breakthrough in individuals, churches
and communities. To God alone be all the glory,
dominion, power, and honor forever and ever.

New Destiny Christian Center P.O. Box 11082 Merrillville,
IN 46410
www.ndccchurch.org
email: ndccchurch@sbcglobal.net
(219) 791-0625

RESTORATION OF GOD'S VESSELS

In the summer of a personally challenging year of my life, Father commissioned me to begin a women's ministry to edify and build up His daughters in Zion. I was slightly hesitant because at that same time my husband felt lead to start a church. I struggled with what I believed God had given me, because of our transition into our own ministry. It seemed such an unethical thing to do, "I am a woman; I am supposed to support my husband. How could Father God give me instructions to do anything else?" This plagued me for a few days, but I eventually yielded to what I had heard and shared it with my husband. He thought it was a good idea and expressed no objections to it whatsoever.

My 'Man of God's' agreement didn't make me any more secure or certain that I was hearing from God. I know that we all get to a place where we have to just trust the voice of God on the inside for ourselves and move forward in faith. Well, this was one of those times for me. Nevertheless, one day as I lay in my bed, I clearly heard the Lord say to me "Call it Women of Destiny' and he led me to the 28th and 29th chapters of II Chronicles. He took me specifically to II Chronicles 28:22-24, *And in the times of his distress did he trespass yet more against the LORD: this is that king Ahaz. For he sacrificed unto the gods of Damascus, which smote him: and he said, Because the gods of the kings of*

Syria help them, therefore will I sacrifice to them, that they may help me. But they were the ruin of him, and of all Israel. And Ahaz gathered together the vessels of the house of God, and cut in pieces the vessels of the house of God, and shut up the doors of the house of the LORD, and he made him altars in every corner of Jerusalem.

My God! These scriptures rang in my spirit like an alarm and I understood Father to instruct me to go, open the doors in the house of God, release His vessels, and bring restoration. Releasing them would not be enough, because of the time period, they had been 'shut up' or shall we say shut down in the house of God. It would require a process of restoration to return them to their proper place and former glory. I had never dwelt on these scriptures before, and neither had I ever related them to the daughters of Zion. It took me some time to adjust to the fact that Father had spoken them from the spirit realm directly into my heart. What a wonderful experience that was. I am sure some of you have experienced it for yourselves. It leaves you with a certainty and assurance that no person, nor teaching, nor book, nor religious rambling, can shake from you.

Without certainty in your spirit that the Lord is speaking to you, men and women (especially women) will attempt to destroy your faith in the Word of freedom that the Lord has delivered to you. I say 'especially women', because on my journey in ministering to women, I have found that women will come against you more than men, to keep themselves and others in bondage. On this commission the Lord has given me, to bring release and restoration to His chosen vessels, the deceptions of the enemy have proven to be stronger than I would have ever imagined. Even after great teachings supported by scripture and sound doctrine, excellent books written by men and women, there are many in the body of Christ who still believe women to be subservient, meaningless females with no other purpose than to serve their husband (maybe yours) or man in general.

This mentality is so against the Word, the wisdom and the will of God. Many men and women in the church still believe Satan's lies that women are second class citizens that have no rights except granted by men. My sisters and brothers, I beseech thee by the mercies of God, not to think of God's daughters in Zion in such a lowly and insulting way. The Bible reads in Psalm 139:14 *I will praise you, for I am fearfully and wonderfully made; marvelous are your works, and my soul knows very well*.

How can a woman, the marvelous work of God, be cast aside as a useless vessel? How can we as citizens of the Kingdom believe that Father God condones bondage of any kind, one creation ruling over another creation; racism, or sexism? We are all citizens of the KINGDOM of GOD, whether we are freeborn or manumitted (freed from slavery), we are free. *If the Son therefore shall make you free, ye shall be free indeed* John 8:36.

The Word says in Genesis 1:27, *So God created man in His own image, in the image of God created he him; male and female created he them*. Woman is created in the image of God, and although she is not the one that opened the matrix (the first born); she is the one that was formed from the one who opened the matrix. In other words, Father God did not create her as an afterthought; she was created with purpose and destiny from and in the beginning. Genesis 5:2 says, *Male and Female created he them; and blessed them, and called their name Adam, in the day when they were created*. The Bible clearly says '*in the day when they were created*'. Woman was not an afterthought; Father God had her in His mind all along when He formed Adam on that day. What a mighty God we serve!! I know, I know, we must mention the fact that Eve (otherwise known as female Adam) was told by God after the fall in the Garden that her desires would be to her husband and he should rule over her, this is found in Genesis 3:16. Yes, this is true, but He never told her she lost her son-ship, her rights, her dominion or her position. He simply told her she would have to yield to her husband and elder brother (in Christ).

112

I say that in a joyful tone, because yielding doesn't mean you are powerless, it simply means you have control over your flesh. Father God told the woman that you did not exercise self- control in the Garden; therefore you will now have to yield to your husband. It was never to become a false doctrine in the church to keep woman bound, so that men could exercise control, manipulation and power over them. It was spoken to Eve, not Adam. She was told from that point on her husband was now her elder, not to be interpreted 'slave master'.

I must bring this to a conclusion, but be it understood my sisters and brothers in Christ, Father God has created Eve in His image, she is His favorite daughter, and He has called for her to be released and restored from the bondages that have been placed on her.
Women of God, obedience and submission are an act of the will, you have rights, and therefore Father encourages you to walk in liberty.
Know that you are loved and you have the power to choose to yield your power to another in love, humility and righteousness.

~~~~

Reflections:

Do you believe that God can use you in ministry? Why / Why not?

_____

_____

_____

What were you raised to believe about women in ministry?

_____

_____

_____

_____

What thoughts or ideas about women still entangle you in your service to God?

_____

_____

_____

Scriptures to Ponder:

Even on my servants, both men and women, I will pour out my Spirit in those days. Joel 2:29

In the last days, God says, I will pour out my Spirit on all people. Your sons and daughters will prophesy, your young men will see visions, your old men will dream dreams. Acts 2:17

After this, Jesus traveled about from one town and village to another, proclaiming the good news of the kingdom of God. The Twelve were with him, [2] and also some women who had been cured of evil spirits and diseases: Mary (called Magdalene) from whom seven demons had come out; [3] Joanna the wife of Chuza, the manager of Herod's household; Susanna; and many others. These women were helping to support them out of their own means. Luke 8:1-3

Chapter 13

Who Can Minister?

By Nina Pringle

Lady Nina Pringle

First Lady Nina Pringle was born in Erin, Tennessee on March 24, 1960, to the parents of Pauline Easley and Leonard Dixon. She later moved to Oakland, California at the age of eight. Being the 5th of 12 children, she was raised with great family values and was blesses to learn how to be a good mother and wife. She married in 1982, a wonderful man, Pastor Casey Pringle and they have 3 beautiful children and 3 grandchildren. Lady Pringle has served the Lord for the past 29 years and am now looking for the Lord to bless her in ministry and writing.

New Testament Church

620 42nd Street

Oakland, California

Who Can Minister?

Naturally speaking, a woman's place in the kingdom of God is by her husband's side living a holy life with him. Man was created to rule and to have dominion over the earth and woman was created to be his help meet.
I Corinthians 11:7-12, *"For a man indeed ought not to cover his head,*
forasmuch as he is the image and glory of God:
but the woman is the glory of the man... Neither
was the man created for the woman; but the
woman for the man... but all things of God." God created us with an inner desire for him and to be of holy comfort and companion to each other. All things in life must be out of our love and relationship with God and our desire to be right in the Lord. We will support and respect each other and work side by side in the Kingdom of God.

When a man and a woman find their place in the kingdom of God, they become blessed of the Lord. Proverbs 18:22 says, *"Whoso findeth a wife findeth a good thing, and obtaineth favor of the Lord."* And 12:4, *"A virtuous woman is a crown to her husband..."* We are to represent the good in each other and stand in support of one another.

It takes a holy man to find his true blessing in the Lord and a holy woman to be the good, virtuous woman and wife that God intended her to be!
God made woman for man's glory and natural

pleasures; her responsibility in the natural is to her husband and family!

To be a woman in the Kingdom of God, we have to be as Titus 2:5 says, *"To be discreet, chaste, keepers at home, good, obedient to their own husbands, that the word of God be not blasphemed."* And Ephesians 5:22-25, *"Wives, submit yourselves unto your own husbands, as unto the Lord... Husbands, love your wives, even as Christ also loved the church, and gave himself for it..."* The relationship between a husband and a wife was intended to be a beautiful, life lasting union.

Sin has caused submission and obedience to be difficult for women to accept; it was not meant to be debasing nor condescending. Women of the Kingdom have a different perspective of submission when men of the Kingdom love them as Christ loved the church and gave his life for it!!! The main reason that the divorce rate is so high is that neither partner has taken the word of God seriously. I Corinthians 7:14 says, *"For the unbelieving husband is sanctified by the wife, and the unbelieving wife is sanctified by the husband..."* You have the responsibility to lead him to the Lord as well as he has to lead you. I knew nothing of the word of God, but through the teaching of my Bishop, the late Casey Pringle; and my Pastor and husband, Casey L. Pringle, Sr., I am saved. I will be forever grateful for what these two men of God have taught me. I have learned by example of my husband how to be sanctified. When I get the opportunity to speak of God's word, it is like "rivers of living water" flowing through me. I cannot contain what I have learned of the Lord and his Word; **I have to tell others of his goodness!**

Jesus brought in Grace and Truth! We as women cannot be saved just because our husbands are saved; our souls have to be holy unto the Lord also. If a woman has a husband that is not living a holy life unto the Lord does that mean that she cannot be saved? Let me be clear, that does not mean that she cannot be saved! Suppose that her husband does not know how to answer her questions regarding the word of God; she has the responsibility to learn what the will of the Lord is for herself.

Though it is widely criticized, women of the Kingdom are taking a stand in the ministry; being filled with the spirit of God makes it difficult not to. Having said that, I do believe that a woman in any position should always remain humble and respectful and not dogmatically exert herself over a man just because she is in authority! I do not agree, that women in the Kingdom should come forward in ministry the way that men do.

We should remain humble and feminine; speaking the truth of God's word in our own characters, establishing a sanctified position before man and God!

God is not pleased with the stereotyped preaching of today. He wants leaders to represent in spirit and truth, teaching his people how to save their lives!

Jeremiah 31:31-34 says,
"Behold, the days come, saith the Lord, that I will make a new covenant with the house of Israel... After those days, saith the Lord, I will put my law in their inward parts, and write it in their hearts; and will be their God, and they shall be my people. And they shall teach no more every man his neighbor, and every man his brother, saying, Know the Lord: for they shall all know me, from the least of them unto the greatest of them, saith the Lord..." This applies to women as well, not just the men, it continues on, *"for they shall all know me, from the least of them unto the greatest of them, saith the Lord..."* God has made a new covenant with the house of Israel, which includes women; he will put his law in our inward parts and our hearts as well! There are a lot of men that call themselves preachers and have received qualifications from theological seminaries, but God said that *He* would send them, that *He* would put his law in their inward parts. These "preachers" do not have the spirit of God because they were not sent by God.

> If a woman opens her heart, mind, and soul for t
> Lord to use her, he will!

Joel 2:28&29 says, *"And it shall come to pass afterward, that I will pour out my spirit upon all flesh; and your sons and your daughters shall prophesy... And also upon the servants and upon the handmaids in those days will I pour out my spirit."*

When God pours out his spirit upon a person, man or woman, they cannot sit still on his word. We have an earnest desire to prophesy of his divine inspiration! We are in that day where God is pouring out his spirit and qualifying women to carry his word. Where she does, it doesn't matter. I have to say, my husband being a pastor, if he dies leaving a strong membership and there is no worthy replacement, I will continue on in leadership. A person converting their soul to the Lord is the absolute best change that anyone can make! If the people of this nation can accept homosexuality (widely accepted in the church); and even pass a law that allows two people of the same sex to marry, my God, ***then why can't we accept a woman of God in leadership?***

I believe that God is well pleased with his women that have come forward to accept him as Lord! We have male Pastors committing adultery, fornication, with evil, lustful desires that are still allowed to be in the pulpit receiving the respect of a Minister. God is certainly not pleased with this and death lies at their door if they don't repent! Women have been used throughout the Bible for various reasons. God has allowed women to work on his behalf to let us know that it is permissible for a woman to have a part in the Kingdom. God will have the last say, it is he that will cast us into the lake of fire or receive us up into his Kingdom.

If God is leading you, he will make a way for you to do his will! Luke 12:31, *"But rather seek ye the kingdom of God; and all these things shall be added unto you. Fear not, little flock; for it is your Father's good pleasure to give you the kingdom."* So, be led by the Lord. Be faithful and true. It is his good pleasure to give you his Kingdom! I have found Matthew 26:10-13 to be very encouraging,

> *"For she hath wrought a good work upon me... Wheresoever this gospel shall be preached in the whole world, there shall also this, that this woman hath done, be told for a memorial of her."*

Jesus was well pleased with this woman; he has made her actions known throughout the world. Women, we can be used by God and God will hold us in high regard in the Kingdom! There is no excuse for anyone to be lost. We were all created by God for his glory as Revelations 4:11 says, *"Thou are worthy, O lord, to receive glory and*

honor and power: for thou hast created all things,
and for thy pleasure they are and were created."

Women were created to give God glory, as well.
We cannot do that if we do not seek him for
ourselves. We have all been called to repentance,
Titus 2:11-14 says, *For the grace of God that*
bringeth salvation hath appeared to all men,
(meaning women too) Teaching us that, denying
ungodliness and worldly lusts, we should live
soberly, righteously, and godly, in this present
world; Looking for that blessed hope, and the
glorious appearing of the great God and our
Savior Jesus Christ..."

We are to live righteously in this present world
looking for that blessed hope, and glorious
appearing of God. We serve a mighty, powerful
God. If he says that we can live holy, redeemed
from all iniquity in this present world, we can!
Spiritually speaking, the Kingdom of God is with
mankind. That means that once we receive the
Holy Ghost spirit of the Lord we dwell in the
Kingdom of God –- Love, Joy, Peace, and the Holy
Ghost! Women, be of good courage, our place in
the Kingdom is in God! James 2:5 says, *"Hath*
not God chosen the poor of this world rich in faith,
and heirs of the kingdom which he hath promised
to them that love him?" Them that love him;
Women and Men, love the Lord your God with all
of your heart, mind, body, and soul, and strength,

and you are guaranteed a place in the Kingdom of God!!!

What's more beautiful is Luke 17:20&21, *"...The kingdom of God cometh not with observation... for, behold, the kingdom of God is within you."* God's spirit dwells within you; allow his love, joy, and peace, to dwell in you richly and you will have found a place in the Kingdom of God!!! I agree with Paul when he said, *"nothing shall separate me from the love of God..."*

We can't allow anything or anybody to take precedence over our love for God!!! May God ever bless you and keep you in his care!

~~~~

Reflections:

Based on righteousness being the standard, are you really qualified for ministry? In what areas do you need to improve?

_____

_____

_____

_____

What do others say about your character?

_____

_____

_____

_____

Scriptures to Ponder:

The nations will see your righteousness, and all kings your glory; you will be called by a new name that the mouth of the LORD will bestow. Isaiah 62:2

God is spirit, and his worshipers must worship
in spirit and in truth.   John 4:24 NIV

The LORD is near to all who call on him, to all
who call on him in truth.
Psalm 145:18 NIV

A wife of noble character who can find? She is worth
far more than rubies. Proverbs 31:10 NIV

Choose one person in scripture. Who do you most
resemble? Why? What are his or her strengths and
weaknesses? What are yours?

_____

_____

_____

_____

_____

_____

_____

Chapter 14

A Woman's Worth

By Apostle Angela Thibeaux

Dr. Angela Thibeaux

Dr. Thibeaux is founder of *His Glory International Covenant Ministries* Church in Chicago, Illinois, *The Apostle's Heartbeat Ministries*, and the recently launched *Kingdom Covenant Ministries,* which offers all the amenities of partnership and outreach.

Dr. Thibeaux is a native of Chicago, IL and resides in the Lake County area with her husband Troy, who is a committed Husband, a loving father and serviceman in the United States Navy, and their four beautiful children Brianna, Brittney, Brandi and Braylon.

Dr. Thibeaux is a veteran of the US Navy During her years as a military spouse she found herself in Yokosuka, Japan where she was birthed into ministry as a preacher of the gospel in 2000 and called to the pastorate in 2002.

His Glory International Covenant Ministries
P.O. Box 434 Round Lake, Illinois 60073
312-852-8828
apostlesheartbeat@hisglory-icm.com
www.hisglory-icm.com

A Woman's Worth

So, God made you a woman. Since He is an all-knowing God, He must have weighed out this decision to create you as a woman against his assigned purpose for your life. He must have considered the obstacles that you would face and the hardships you would endure to fulfill His purpose and He still created you woman. Either this is some sick joke or He is infinitely wise, strategically graceful and confidently rules. He wouldn't create you as woman then give you gifts that draw you toward a destiny not accessible to you. He wouldn't make you a woman then call you into the depths of His presence, allow His anointing to pour over you, reveal Himself and His mysteries, then say "Don't speak because you're a woman." As women in the Kingdom of God we must reconcile our lives with the truth of God. Who are we? Why were we created? How do we add value to the Kingdom?

The worth (value) of the woman has been removed, ignored, devalued, and trampled upon for generations. If a person, not just women, does not know its own worth or identity they will relinquish their personal value, purpose achievement, and life fulfillment. When this happens it not only affects the individual but those directly or indirectly associated with them. Christ's knowledge of His worth and identity is what lead Him to the cross and has affected the life and destiny of every human being, those that have received salvation and those who have not. So, to understand worth pertaining to the woman we must seek the truth that can only be discovered in who God is and the mysteries of His purpose.

This topic of woman in respects to worth (value) has been approached from many angles, yet not completely understood. Many have tried to bottle a woman's worth to merely being creatures created to produce children, hold domestic duties, and to serve her husband and children. Although all of these are true, they are also incomplete. To tell women this, is a lie that speaks contrary to God's creative authority.

Webster's Dictionary defines Worth as:

1. Equal in value to (in comparison to another object)
2. Deserving of (declared worthy to receive something due to works or qualities it possess)
3. Monetary value (assessed by an economic authority which determines an amount based upon supply and demand)
4. Moral or personal merit

Strong's Complete Dictionary of Bible Words defines Worth as:

1. Like, as; for; with (in comparison to)
2. Price, payment, wages (assessed monetary value)
3. Valuation of a thing (deserving of)
4. Full; filling; fullness; fully. Accomplish. The verb generally denotes the completion of

something that was unfinished or the filling of something that was empty.

Both the Webster's and the Strong's definitions are similar at a glance but when you take a closer look you will discover that part of the meaning of this word has been overlooked. As we see in Strong's fourth definition, worth cannot be determined without considering the full measure or capability of what or who is being evaluated. Many have used the example of a top of the line vehicle being considered for purchase. This vehicle offers supreme parts, features, and benefits that add to its value, making it worth spending top dollar to purchase. Now its creator and economic experts access a price value according to the knowledge of how it was created and the need for its supply. Once the vehicle is purchased it is up to the purchaser to realize the value, maximize on the benefits and enjoy all the features. If the purchaser does not do so by choice or ignorance, it does not decrease the value of the vehicle. It only means that the purchaser will miss out on the full value of the vehicle. Our creator has not diminished the value of women in the kingdom even though some do not fully grasp their worth to the kingdom.

Women have been given gifts, talents, abilities and authority. James 1:17 says, *Every good gift and every perfect gift is from above, and cometh down from the Father of lights with whom is no variableness, neither shadow of turning.* James let's us know that every bit of good in us comes from the giver, our Father of illumination and revealing. He does not change nor turn from what He declared from the time in which we were created (Num 23:19; 1Sam 15:29; Mal 3:6; Rom 11:29). If the good in us is of the Lord then what are we to do with it if not to share it with those in need?

Our worth is not predicated upon mans determination of value but only God himself our creator and economic assessor can determine that. We must seek him to understand who we are. I believe David asked this question better than any of us as he asked, *"Who is man (mortals) that thou art mindful of him? And the son of man (male and female, mankind), that thou visitest him? For thou hast made him a little lower than the angels, and hast crowned him with glory and honor. Thou madest him to have dominion over the works of thy hands: thou hast put all things under his feet: All sheep and oxen, yea, and the beasts of the field; the fowl of the air, and the fish of the sea, and whatsoever passeth through the paths of the seas. O Lord our Lord, how excellent is thy name in all thy earth! (Ps 8:4-9)*

This is an age old question that people ask themselves everyday. We seek to knowwho we are, why were we born and what should we do with our lives. God is the only one able to answer this question with the whole truth. Unfortunately we have looked for answers in all the wrong resources. Our worth and identity is not based on the external things but wholly based on our spiritual DNA. Our identity and worth is based on who God is. He stated that everything he created was good and he blessed the works of his hands. No longer can the kingdom afford for women to not know their value or not fulfill his purpose for their lives. We were made in his image and that image is the only thing that shuts down the forces of darkness and evokes heaven to move. Our place in the kingdom is to fulfill the will of our father, to live transformed lives and advance the cause of the kingdom by spreading the Gospel message in word and deed. Women today that know their God and embrace who they are in him are rising to purpose and fearlessly advancing the kingdom. We are wholly being restored as Proverbs 31 women of prayer and power. Our voices are being heard across the world, heralding the message of the Kingdom. We are valuable and necessary to kingdom advancement.

As the kingdom is being revealed, the more we will see all persons being called to purpose and women will hear the call and say, "Yes."

~~~

Reflections:

Who are you?

_____

_____

_____

_____

Do you see yourself as valuable to the Kingdom? Why or Why not?

_____

_____

_____

_____

_____

_____

What is your worth based upon?

_____

_____

_____

_____

God has given you gifts. What will you do with them?

_____

_____

_____

_____

_____

_____

Scriptures to Ponder:

Bring all who claim me as their God, for I have made them for my glory. It was I who created them. Isaiah 43:7

For we are God's workmanship, created in Christ Jesus to do good works, which God prepared in advance for us to do.   Ephesians 2:10 NIV

Dear Reader,

All of the contributing women to this project have committed a part of themselves to help all those who dare read this book. We've shared the word that God gave us to give to you. We have prayed for you. We trust that something in this book will touch your soul; even if it's just one sharing.

May you open up your heart and mind to reach your God-ordained destiny. Begin your amazing journey today. There are great things in line for your future.

The Lord wants you to understand that there is a place for you in His Kingdom. He has not given you gifts and then forbidden you to use them. That is inconsistent with his Word.

Receive the message of this book and if you aren't fully convinced, go deeper. Study for yourself. Take an objective journey through the Word. Ask the Holy Spirit to be your guide. He will honor such a noble request.

The Lord wants you to be free to soar into purpose.

Sincerely,

Crystal Jones & Joceline Bronson, Publishers
Destiny House Publishing, LLC
www.destinyhousepublishing.com

Other Books Published by
Destiny House Publishing, LLC

Barren, But Pregnant with Promise
by Joceline Bronson

Broken To Worship by Janice Townsend

Creating A Brat-Free Home by BJ Harris

Diary of A Broken Praise Dancer by Aries Winans

Memoirs of A Phenomenal Woman
Compiled by Bessie Sims

The S Word: What Submission Is Not
By Crystal Jones

The Tabernacle: A Journey of Faith
by Kristen Tschida

Made in the USA
Charleston, SC
27 December 2012